THE MILITARY EXPERIENCE.
IN THE AIR:
FIGHTER JETS

THE MILITARY EXPERIENCE.

IN THE AIR: FIGHTER JETS

JIM CORRIGAN

MORGAN REYNOLDS
PUBLISHING

GREENSBORO, NORTH CAROLINA

 To join the discussion about this title, please check out the Morgan Reynolds Readers Club on Facebook, or Like our company page to stay up to date on the latest Morgan Reynolds news!

For
Captain Michael Scott Speicher,
a Navy F/A-18 pilot who was shot down
and killed during the early hours of
Operation Desert Storm

Lockheed Martin F-22A Raptor

The Military Experience.
In the Air: Fighter Jets
Copyright © 2014 by Morgan Reynolds Publishing

Library of Congress Cataloging-in-Publication Data

Corrigan, Jim.
  Fighter jets / by Jim Corrigan.
      pages cm. -- (The military experience. In the air)
  Includes bibliographical references and index.
  ISBN 978-1-59935-376-0 -- ISBN 978-1-59935-377-7 (e-book) 1.
Fighter
planes. 2. Fighter plane combat. I. Title.
  UG1242.F5C678 2013
  358.4'383--dc23

                    2013007131

Printed in the United States of America
First Edition

Book cover and interior designed by:
Ed Morgan, navyblue design studio
Greensboro, NC

Table of Contents

READY
to Adapt

CHAPTER ONE

A U.S. Air Force Block 40 F-16 Fighting Falcon

The day began like no other. It was September 11, 2001.

"We have some planes," a strange voice announced over the air traffic control radio.

The chilling message came from a terrorist who was sitting in the cockpit of a jumbo airliner.

Twenty minutes later, a Boeing 767 streaked over New York City and slammed into the World Trade Center's North Tower. Within moments, another hijacked 767 sliced across the skyline, striking the South Tower. Fires raged, and soon both buildings buckled and collapsed.

Meanwhile, in Washington, D.C., the Pentagon was ablaze. Terrorists had steered a Boeing 757 into the iconic military headquarters. Suddenly, America's skies seemed ominous and threatening. Nobody knew how many more hijacked airliners were out there, or where they might strike.

World Trade Center
September 11, 2001

An F-16 flying in Iraq

AN IMPOSSIBLE SACRIFICE

At nearby Andrews Air Force Base, Lieutenant Heather Penney scrambled toward her F-16 fighter jet. She and her commander, Colonel Marc Sasseville, had just been given an astonishing, deadly mission. Another hijacked 757 was hurtling through the sky, and it was heading toward the nation's capital. These two fighter pilots were ordered to intercept it and, if necessary, bring it down.

There was a huge problem. The 9/11 terrorists achieved such total surprise that no armed fighter jets were ready. Loading the sophisticated F-16s with bullets and missiles would take nearly an hour, which was much too long. By then, the hijacked airliner might have already reached its target. The only way to stop it would be to ram it. In other words, the F-16 pilots would be trying for a deadly midair collision.

As Sasseville and Penney grabbed their flight gear, Sasseville said, "I'm going to go for the cockpit."

"I'll take the tail," Penney replied.

"Let's go!"

Minutes later, they were speeding down the runway, lifting off into a stark blue sky. The F-16s turned northwest and roared ahead at more than four-hundred miles (644 kilometers) per hour. Below them, the Pentagon billowed black smoke. This morning's events, and their current mission, were almost too incredible to believe. But fighter pilots are trained to adapt and remain calm in any situation. The airliner was still far away but they were closing on it rapidly.

As a young girl, Penney never imagined she would one day pilot a fighter jet. She learned about airplanes from her father, who flew jets in the Vietnam War. She even earned her civilian pilot's license while still in college. Back in those days, the U.S. military forbade women from flying combat missions. When that policy finally changed in the mid-1990s, Penney was among the first to sign up.

"I wanted to be a fighter pilot like my dad," she later told the *Washington Post*.

Marine F-4J Phantom II fighters and Red Devils being refueled on a trans-Pacific flight around 1972

Of the hundreds of military aviators who earn their wings each year, only the very best go on to become fighter pilots. Penney was one of those talented and determined few. She endured rigorous training, and slowly earned the respect of her male peers. They gave her a call sign, or nickname, that fit well with her last name. Upon graduation, Lieutenant Heather "Lucky" Penney was assigned to an F-16 fighter squadron.

Now, she found herself racing to intercept a hijacked airliner, possibly crashing into it to save lives on the ground. She thought of ejecting just before impact but then dismissed the idea. She could not chance her plane missing its target.

FAST fact

The U.S. Air Force currently has more than seven-hundred female pilots and sixty female combat pilots. In 2012, Colonel Jeannie Flynn Leavitt became the first female wing commander, overseeing 5,000 airmen at Seymour Johnson Air Force Base in North Carolina.

THE FIRST LINE OF DEFENSE

As it turned out, thanks to the bravery of others, she never had to try. Before the F-16s arrived, some courageous passengers prevented their hijackers from going any further. They rose up and stormed the cockpit. The terrorists, before losing control, nosed the airliner down and flew straight into the ground, killing all aboard.

"The real heroes are the passengers on Flight 93 who were willing to sacrifice themselves," Penney later reflected. "I was just an accidental witness to history."

The two fighter pilots were ordered to remain in the air. President George W. Bush was returning to Washington aboard Air Force One, and the F-16s pulled alongside as an escort.

That evening, and for days after, fighter jets patrolled the skies, guarding against further threats and assuring Americans that they were protected. Soon many of those same aircraft would be headed overseas. The 9/11 terrorist attacks triggered two distant wars, in Afghanistan and Iraq. In both, U.S. airpower would prove essential. As always, fighter jets led the way.

Flight 93 crashed in Pennsylvania.

FAST fact

Today, armed fighter jets are always on standby to defend U.S. airspace.

A ground crew member signals to the pilot of a 614th Tactical Fighter Squadron F-16C Fighting Falcon aircraft.

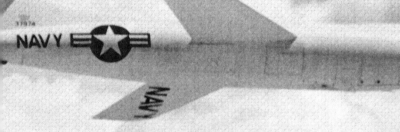

CHAPTER TWO

Evolution of a KILLER

This mid-1950s photograph shows the Douglas D-558-2 and the North American F-86 Sabre chase aircraft in flight.

The Royal Air Force pilot kept his de Havilland Mosquito straight and level. Below him passed a neat patchwork of green and brown squares, the farms of southern Germany. It was 1944, during the waning months of World War II.

The RAF pilot was flying a reconnaissance mission. He did not fear attack; American and British fighters long ago chased enemy aircraft from this region. His Mosquito ambled along as cameras in its belly photographed the German landscape.

Suddenly, a gray blur streaked past. The pilot watched awestruck as this mysterious aircraft turned sharply and circled back. It was a German fighter, he realized, but like none he had ever seen before. It was sleek and menacing, and instead of propellers, it had two torpedo-shaped engines. The British pilot was staring at an Me 262—the world's first fighter jet. And it was coming straight for him.

He ducked into a bank of cumulus clouds as the jet opened fire. After several tense moments, he emerged to find no trace of the jet, and warily turned his Mosquito for home. A new era in air warfare had just begun, and he was relieved to be alive to tell about it.

A German Me 262 in March 1945

An afterburner glows on an
F-15 Eagle engine.

FAST
fact

A propeller chops through
the air, pulling the airplane
forward. A jet engine sucks in air, mixes
it with fuel and ignites it, then expels
the mix as a high-speed gas. This
creates tremendous thrust that pushes
the airplane forward.

Soviet groundcrew prepare a MiG-15.

THE RULERS OF THE SKY

For the remainder of World War II, Me 262s buzzed over Germany like angry bees, but there were too few to make a difference. America and Britain sent thousands of slower, propeller-driven fighters and bombers, and they attacked relentlessly until the war finally ended. But the jet engine's value was obvious to everyone. Within just a few years, fighter jets would rule the sky.

American fighter jets first flew into combat during the Korean War (1950-1953). Korea was the opening battleground of the Cold War, a decades-long rivalry between the United States and the Soviet Union. America was protecting South Korea from invasion by communist North Korea. The Soviets, meanwhile, provided North Korea with weapons including their new fighter jet, the MiG-15. China joined the war as a North Korean ally, and Chinese pilots also flew the MiG-15.

FAST fact

"MiG" is short for Mikoyan and Gurevich, two engineers who founded the Soviet Union's aircraft-design bureau.

American aviators soon found themselves outnumbered by enemy aircraft, especially along the Chinese-Korean border, a deadly strip of airspace they nicknamed MiG Alley. It was here that the first jet-versus-jet air battles took place. They were vicious dogfights of high-speed twists and turns, as desperate foes angled to catch each other in their gun-sights. America's new F-86 Sabre proved an effective match for the MiG-15, and pilots on both sides scored enough kills to become aces.

F-86 Sabres during the Korean War at Suwon Air Base, South Korea

Frenchman Adolphe Pégoud, the "first ace," being awarded the *Croix de guerre*

FAST fact

A pilot needs five aerial victories to earn the honorary title of ace.

By the time America entered the Vietnam War (1959-1975), air-to-air missiles had changed the nature of dogfighting. A pilot could now shoot an enemy aircraft without ever seeing it. Engineers grew so confident in missiles that they designed the F-4 Phantom with no guns. Combat pilots who first flew the F-4 were furious. If a missile missed, its target would draw too close for another launch, making old-fashioned dogfighting necessary. The pilots demanded guns, and soon new Phantoms coming off the assembly line carried a twenty millimeter cannon.

A U.S. Marine Corps McDonnell F-4B-27-MC Phantom II

AIR SUPPORT

Missiles were not only a powerful new weapon but a dangerous threat. North Vietnam's small air force could not stop the swarms of American fighters and bombers overhead, so it invested heavily in surface-to-air missiles (SAMs). Fast-moving SAMs rose up out of the jungle without warning, honing in on a jet's radar reflection or heat signature. Pilots developed tricks and tools for avoiding SAMs. They dropped flares to confuse heat-seeking missiles, and deployed chaff—a cloud of metallic confetti—to interfere with a missile's radar guidance. Regardless, SAMs claimed 110 U.S. Air Force aircraft over Vietnam.

The SAM threat came just as fighter jets were flying closer to the ground than ever, to support soldiers in firefights. Enemy troops were experts at ambush and other guerrilla tactics. They emerged ghostlike from the jungle to launch ferocious attacks on American patrols and bases. Fighter pilots adapted to this new style of warfare, striking enemy positions with bombs, rockets, and a jellied gasoline called napalm.

Napalm bombs explode on Vietcong structures south of Saigon in the Republic of Vietnam.

This type of mission, called close air support, remained a vital part of U.S. military strategy long after South Vietnam fell. Designers realized that future fighter jets would need to be good at more than just dogfighting. The era of the multi-role fighter was about to begin.

FAST
fact

· · · · · · · · · · · · · ·

Historians classify America's long line of fighter jets by generation. Early models—such as those that fought in Korea—were first-generation fighters. The Vietnam War began with second-generation fighters. Before it ended, new technology gave rise to a third generation of jets, such as the F-4 Phantom. Most fighters flying today are fourth generation, but the new F-22 Raptor and F-35 Lightning II are considered fifth-generation fighter jets.

· · · · · · · · · · · · · ·

Two F-22A Raptors in column flight

CHAPTER THREE
MISSIONS and TACTICS

A pilot and a three-ship formation of F-15E Strike Eagles

THE MILITARY EXPERIENCE.

In January 1991, a crisis was unfolding in the Middle East.

Five months earlier, Iraq invaded its tiny neighbor, the oil-rich kingdom of Kuwait. The United Nations (UN) condemned the invasion and ordered Iraq to leave by January 15, but this deadline passed with Iraqi troops still entrenched firmly in Kuwait. The world watched and waited for a UN response.

Operation Desert Storm began in the early morning darkness of January 17, 1991. Hundreds of UN-coalition aircraft, led by American fighter jets, converged on Iraq and Kuwait. They destroyed Iraqi aircraft and missile sites, knocked out electricity and communications, and pounded Iraqi troop strongholds. The massive air assault lasted five and a half weeks, crippling Iraq's ability to wage war. When it finally ended, UN-coalition ground forces moved in. They needed just one-hundred hours to liberate Kuwait and push the Iraqis deep inside their own territory. Airpower had paved the way.

Eagle F-15Es fly over Kuwaiti oil fires, set by the retreating Iraqi army during Operation Desert Storm.

A right side view of a Fighter Squadron 126 (VF-126)
TA-4F Skyhawk aircraft parked on the flight line

NEW TARGETS, NEW STRATEGIES

Before the Vietnam War, fighter jets were built primarily for dogfighting.
(Jets designed for ground attack received an "A" designation, such as the A-4
Skyhawk or A-6 Intruder.) But the guerrilla nature of Vietnam showed that
fighters needed to be more flexible. After winning the skies over a war zone,
they could also help win battles on the ground. Accordingly, in the 1970s,
aircraft manufacturers began building multi-role fighters, complex jets
capable of a variety of missions. Their overwhelming success in Operation
Desert Storm ensured that multi-role fighter jets were here to stay.

A MULTI-ROLE FIGHTER

The F-15 Eagle was originally designed for dogfighting, or air superiority, as evidenced by its huge wing surfaces and twin engines. But the Air Force told manufacturer McDonnell Douglas to also add a ground-attack capability. When the first F-15 lifted off in 1972, it was not only an elite dogfighter, it could also carry eighteen 500 pounds (227 kilograms) bombs. Since then, McDonnell Douglas has continuously added new and better versions, including the F-15E Strike Eagle, a true multi-role fighter that can fly missions in the worst weather.

The Strike Eagle has a two-person aircrew. Directly behind the pilot sits the weapons systems officer, or WSO, a highly trained specialist who handles many elements of the plane's operation. WSO Al Gale was in his Strike Eagle over Iraq during the first night of Operation Desert Storm. Twenty years later, he told aviation author Steve Davies what it felt like to be at the leading edge of a war:

> We all were on the terrain following radar at 200 feet [61 meters] in radio silence. As we flew along . . . we would pass over cars traveling on the highway sometimes. It looked just like any highway at night. It felt strange to know that those drivers who must have heard us going by at over 500 knots were just driving along watching jets with a total of over 200 bombs to drop on their military.

An F-15E Strike Eagle

THE VIPER

There were plenty of F-16s in the air that night, too. Smaller and lighter than an Eagle, the sleek F-16 was built for speed and agility. Officially it's the Fighting Falcon, but pilots call it the Viper because it reminds them of the fictional starfighter from the TV show *Battlestar Galactica*.

The Viper's ability to travel at twice the speed of sound makes it ideal for a special combat mission known as Wild Weasel. Key targets such as airbases and command bunkers are usually heavily defended by SAMs and anti-aircraft artillery. Wild Weasels hunt down these defenses. Before an airstrike, three or four F-16s will sweep onto the target scene and cause havoc, like a weasel in a hen house. They draw heavy fire and knock out missile batteries, enabling bombers to move in and destroy the target.

FAST fact

After firing a missile, fighter pilots typically turn hard in another direction because the missile's smoke trail reveals their location, making them a target.

"SAM hunting is the most dangerous mission faced by today's fighter pilots," says retired Viper pilot Dan Hampton, "a job more hazardous and difficult than shooting down enemy jets." Hampton flew a variety of F-16 missions, but Wild Weasel was always his favorite. "It's where the action is," he says. Hampton has been credited with destroying twenty-one SAM sites during his career, plus many more tanks, trucks, artillery, and aircraft on the ground.

CBU-24 cluster bombs fitted to a US Air Force F-105 Wild Weasel

F/A-18 Super Hornets

THE HORNET

Since 1983, the F/A-18 Hornet has been roaming the world's seas aboard American aircraft carriers. The Hornet's unique Fighter/Attack designation reflects its proficiency at both dogfighting and ground attack. It was also the first fully digital fighter jet, with a core mission computer that displays a wealth of cockpit data about the plane's status and tactical situation. In 1999, an upgraded version called the Super Hornet came into service. It is larger and heavier than the original Hornet, and it carries more fuel for greater range.

HIGH SPEED PRECISION

Fighter jets need airport-length runways for takeoffs and landings, but a Navy fighter doesn't have that luxury. Navy jets must use only the deck of an aircraft carrier—roughly three football fields—for takeoffs and landings. They launch with the aid of a steam-powered catapult that flings them into the air at more than 150 miles per hour (241 kilometers per hour).

An F/A-18 Hornet launches from the flight deck of a conventionally powered aircraft carrier.

FAST
fact

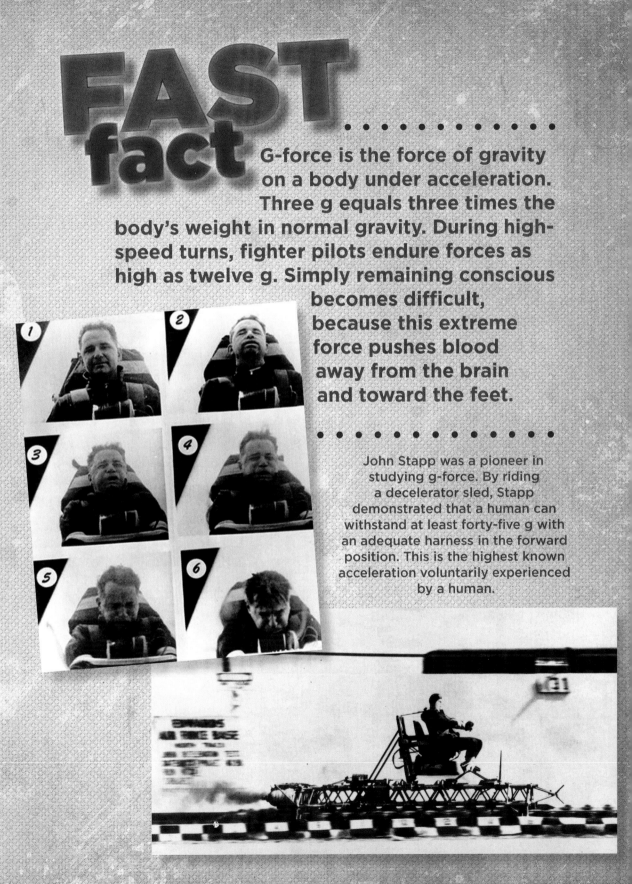

G-force is the force of gravity on a body under acceleration. Three g equals three times the body's weight in normal gravity. During high-speed turns, fighter pilots endure forces as high as twelve g. Simply remaining conscious becomes difficult, because this extreme force pushes blood away from the brain and toward the feet.

John Stapp was a pioneer in studying g-force. By riding a decelerator sled, Stapp demonstrated that a human can withstand at least forty-five g with an adequate harness in the forward position. This is the highest known acceleration voluntarily experienced by a human.

Landings, or recoveries, are even more dramatic. A pilot must carefully descend toward the carrier's runway, which is often pitching and rolling from the motion of the sea. He or she tries to snag the plane's tailhook on one of four steel cables stretched across the runway. If successful, the plane is yanked to a complete stop. A miss means that the pilot must instantly fire up the engines, take off, and circle around for another attempt. Carrier landings, particularly at night and in heavy seas, are some of the most amazing feats in military aviation. Even during peacetime, Navy pilots must adapt to ever-changing variables.

No matter the jet or branch of service, all pilots rely on their ground crews, expert technicians who keep these intricate machines flying at peak performance. Fighter pilots also rely on each other. Large missions can involve dozens or even hundreds of aircraft, but for fighter pilots it all comes down to a basic team of two: the flight leader and his wingman.

A crew monitors the approach path and arresting gear equipment of an EA-6B Prowler before it lands on the flight deck aboard USS *George Washington* in 2004.

FAST fact

Precision aerobatic teams perform at airshows across the country and around the world, serving as military ambassadors of goodwill. The Air Force Thunderbirds fly F-16s, while the Navy Blue Angels take to the skies in F/A-18s.

The Blue Angels

CHAPTER FOUR
Flight
LEADER
&Wingman

Air-to-air right side view of an USAF T-38 Talon aircraft as his wingman banks to the left

Fighter pilots spend their whole careers learning to get better.

In the ever evolving world of air combat, it seems there is always a new school to attend, a new skill to acquire. This culture of constant learning keeps pilots sharp and ready to adapt.

A rookie who has just earned his or her wings still has many months of advanced training to pass before being assigned to a fighter squadron. There are combat tactics to learn in the air, and survival techniques to learn on the ground. And upon finally reaching a squadron, this outstanding pilot with years of training is still considered just a rookie. The pilot still has much to learn. He or she becomes a wingman.

The concept of the wingman is as old as dogfighting itself, and it's more than just a way to train rookie pilots. In the air, where a threat may come from any angle, it is far better to have two sets of eyes on alert rather than just one. Fighter pilots almost always work in pairs, with the more experienced aviator leading the way. The flight leader assumes responsibility for success of the mission, and more important, for the safety of his wingman. Veteran flight leaders sometimes command a four-plane flight, an even greater challenge.

A Blue Angels wingman

THE MISSION BEGINS

Typical missions begin in the briefing room, where flight leader and wingman go over all the details: target data, attack plan, weather forecast, refueling points, and much more. Dan Hampton, the retired Wild Weasel flight leader, said that a thorough mission briefing lasts about ninety minutes. "Contingencies and how to deal with them at five hundred knots, when people are shooting at you, are a major point of discussion," he explains. "*Everything* bad that could happen can't be addressed, of course, but the main idea is to have plans that will adapt and work."

Fighter jets loaded down with bombs and missiles burn a large amount of fuel during takeoff, so usually the first task once airborne is to top off their fuel tanks. Aerial refueling is a delicate procedure requiring the pilot to fly straight and steady behind a large tanker plane. An operator aboard the tanker extends a telescoping tube called the boom, gently guiding it to a small port on the fighter. "In peacetime, there's lots of talk back and forth between the boomer and the receiving pilot," notes Hampton, "but in combat, there's none."

Combat pilots always assume enemy radio operators are listening in, so they talk only when necessary and use code words. ("Magnum" and "Slapshot" are code words for firing a missile at a SAM site.) Flight leader and wingman often reply to each other by simply clicking the microphone button several times, a technique called "zippering the mike."

FAST fact

An AWACS plane is an airborne air-traffic controller. A large transport plane fitted with powerful radar, it orbits high above the combat zone, furnishing pilots with mission updates, and maintaining order among the many aircraft in the area. AWACS stands for Airborne Warning and Control System.

A Lockheed P-3B Orion AEW of the U.S. Customs and Border Protection service in flight

F-15 flying vertically, releasing flares

COMBAT!

With their fuel tanks full, the fighter jets speed off toward their target. If they run into an enemy fighter along the way, the flight leader and wingman might suddenly dart in opposite directions. This tactic forces their adversary to pursue one plane, leaving him open to attack by the other.

In recent wars, American pilots have encountered little to no resistance from enemy fighters. During the opening days of Operation Desert Storm, three dozen Iraqi pilots took off only to be shot down almost immediately. The rest fled to neighboring Iran for safety. Following the 9/11 terrorist attacks, as U.S. forces invaded Afghanistan and later returned to Iraq, American fighter jets roamed the skies unchallenged. This kind of air dominance allows fighter pilots to focus entirely on ground targets.

The big question for the future is whether U.S. fighter jets will be able to maintain their tremendous advantage. Other nations are currently building advanced fighters that could challenge American air dominance. In a future war, a flight leader and his wingman might suddenly discover that they are not the hunters but the hunted.

FAST fact

No enemy pilot has ever shot down an American F-15 Eagle, while Eagles have downed 107 enemy planes to date.

CHAPTER FIVE

The FUTURE

An F/A-22 Raptor flies a training mission over California.

They call it the Mighty Dragon, and it glides through the sky like a ferocious predator.

The fighter jet has stealth technology to hide from radar, and broad wings that sweep back to its twin engines. Near the cockpit a secondary set of wings protrude menacingly. Known as canards, they give the Mighty Dragon added agility.

The J-20, which made its first flight in January 2011, was designed by the Chengdu Aircraft Industry Group. So far, Chengdu has built only a few prototypes, or test planes. But soon it will likely begin mass-producing the J-20 for the Chinese People's Liberation Army Air Force.

During the Cold War, Soviet jets like the MiG-29 posed a serious challenge to American airpower. After the Soviet Union collapsed in 1991, U.S. fighters reigned supreme. That's all changing now, as emerging nations like China develop their own advanced fighters. None of these new players are hostile toward America, but nobody can predict the future of international relations. The J-20 Mighty Dragon and others like it could easily outperform an F-15, F-16, or F/A-18.

An artist's rendering of the Chengdu J-20

F-22 Raptor

THE NEXT GENERATION

The good news is that America's next generation of jet fighters is already here. The F-22 Raptor came into service in 2005. Pilots marvel at the Raptor's speed and maneuverability, and its dynamic cockpit displays and controls. Like all stealth aircraft, the Raptor has a sharply angled airframe to deflect enemy radar beams. Its skin is radar-absorbent, and while non-stealth fighters carry bombs and missiles under their wings, a Raptor stores its weapons internally.

"It's the fighter aircraft fighter pilots have been dreaming about," said Lieutenant Colonel Mike "Dozer" Shower. "It's an absolute thoroughbred for raw power and speed."

The problem with the F-22 is its price tag: a staggering $150 million per plane. The U.S. Air Force hoped to buy nearly four-hundred Raptors, enough to replace the aging F-15 Eagle. Ultimately, it could afford only about half that many, meaning the F-15 will remain in service. Future dogfights will likely feature Raptors and Eagles flying together as a team.

FAST
fact

The revolutionary F-117 Nighthawk was strictly a ground-attack aircraft. Early stealth technology enabled it to elude radar as it delivered laser-guided bombs deep inside enemy territory. The Air Force retired the F-117 in 2008.

F-117 Nighthawk

Another elite fighter is on the horizon—the F-35 Lightning II. (It's also called the Joint Strike Fighter because America is developing it jointly with the United Kingdom and other close allies.) The highly adaptable F-35 will come in three different versions. The first model will take off and land using a traditional runway, the second will be able to land vertically like a helicopter, and the third will be suited to an aircraft carrier. Prototypes of all three versions are currently making test flights.

British test pilot Graham "GT" Tomlinson explained that the Lightning differs from its big brother, the Raptor. He said that the F-35 "was designed to be a jack of all trades, and is not going to be better than the F-22 in dogfighting." However, Tomlinson believes the Lightning will outshine the Raptor in ground-attack missions like hunting down SAMs. "The F-35 is going to be by far the best choice of aircraft for the first few days of any future war, when we will need to stealthily destroy the enemy's air defenses," he said.

FAST fact

Thanks to U.S. fighter jets, no American ground soldier has died at the hands of an enemy pilot since the Korean War. It is unclear whether U.S. fighters will be able to maintain this air dominance in future wars.

F-35 in flight

The Lightning's financial cost has climbed much higher than originally projected, a difficult problem that is delaying its production. Cost is always an issue with next-generation fighter jets. They are among the most advanced aircraft ever built, requiring years of research and testing. Even during peacetime, they demand constant maintenance and care.

Yet no modern military can succeed without them. They lead the way into battle, clearing away obstacles to victory and protecting troops on the ground. Like the men and women who fly them, fighter jets adapt to any challenge.

FAST fact

Drones, or remotely piloted aircraft, now fly some missions once reserved for fighters. Drones can provide surveillance of enemy activity and even fire missiles. In 2012, the U.S. Air Force trained more drone pilots than fighter and bomber pilots.

A MQ-9 Reaper (drone) flies above Creech Air Force Base during a local training mission

Sources

Chapter 1: Ready to Adapt

p. 12,   "We have some planes," National Commission on Terrorist Attacks, *The 9/11 Commission Report: Final Report of the National Commission on Terrorist Attacks Upon the United States* (New York: W.W. Norton, 2004), 10.

p. 13,   "I'm going to go . . ." Steve Hendrix, "F-16 Pilot Was Ready to Give Her Life on Sept. 11," *Washington Post*, September 8, 2011.

p. 14,   "I wanted to be . . ." Ibid.

p. 16,   "The real heroes are the . . ." Ibid.

Chapter 3: Missions and Tactics

p. 32,   "We all were on the terrain . . ." Steve Davies, *U.S. Multi-Role Fighter Jets* (New York: Osprey Publishing, 2011), 45.

p. 34,   "SAM hunting is the most . . ." Dan Hampton, *Viper Pilot: A Memoir of Air Combat* (New York: HarperCollins, 2012), 14.

p. 34,   "It's where the action is," Ibid.

Chapter 4: Flight Leader & Wingman

p. 44,   "Contingencies and how to deal . . ." Hampton, *Viper Pilot*, 58.

p. 44,   "In peacetime, there's lots . . ." Ibid., 188.

Chapter 5: The Future

p. 51,   "It's the fighter aircraft . . ." Davies, *U.S. Multi-Role Fighter Jets*, 194.

p. 53,   "was designed to be a jack . . ." Ibid., 212.

Glossary

airframe: The framework and skin of an aircraft.

boom: A telescoping tube that airborne tankers use to refuel other aircraft.

call sign: A pilot's nickname, usually given by other pilots.

canard: A small wing located in front of the main wings.

chaff: Strips of metal foil dropped by an aircraft to confuse enemy radar.

close air support: A mission against enemy targets that are near friendly ground forces.

guerrilla: A style of warfare using ambushes, raids, and sabotage.

multi-role: A term given to fighters capable of flying a variety of missions.

prototype: An experimental model; the first of its kind.

reconnaissance: A search of terrain for militarily useful information.

SAM (surface-to-air missile): An anti-aircraft missile guided by radar or heat sensors.

stealth: an aircraft's ability to avoid radar and heat detection.

squadron: a basic unit of military aircraft.

tailhook: A device for making aircraft carrier landings and other short landings.

Wild Weasel: A mission to destroy enemy missile batteries and other air defenses.

wing commander: A high-ranking officer in charge of an air base.

WSO (weapon systems officer): A flight specialist who sits behind the pilot in some fighter jets.

Bibliography

Anderton, David A. *The History of the U.S. Air Force.* New York: Crescent Books, 1981.

Bowden, Mark. "The Last Ace." http://www.theatlantic.com/magazine/archive/2009/03/the-last-ace/307291.

Chivers, C.J. "Afghan Conflict Losing Air Power as U.S. Pulls Out." *New York Times,* July 6, 2012.

Davies, Steve. *U.S. Multi-Role Fighter Jets.* New York: Osprey Publishing, 2011.

Hampton, Dan. *Viper Pilot: A Memoir of Air Combat.* New York: HarperCollins, 2012.

Hendrix, Steve. "F-16 Pilot Was Ready to Give Her Life on Sept. 11." *Washington Post,* September 8, 2011.

Michaels, Jim. "Drones Change 'Top Gun' Culture of Air Force." *USA Today,* December 1, 2012.

National Commission on Terrorist Attacks. *The 9/11 Commission Report: Final Report of the National Commission on Terrorist Attacks Upon the United States.* New York: W.W. Norton, 2004.

Raddatatz, Martha. "Female Fighter Pilot Breaks Gender Barriers." http://abcnews.go.com/blogs/headlines/2012/10/female-fighter-pilot-breaks-gender-barriers.

Rendall, Ivan. *Rolling Thunder: Jet Combat from World War II to the Gulf War.* New York: The Free Press, 1997.

Talmadge, Eric. "Insurgents Push Fighter Pilots to New Tactics." http://www.airforcetimes.com/news/2007/07/ap_fighterpilots_070704.

Web sites

Assessing China's J-20 Mighty Dragon
http://media.aerosociety.com/aerospace-insight/2011/01/14/not-so-hidden-dragon-j-20-assessed/3524/

F-22 Raptor: A Fifth-Generation Fighter
http://www.f22-raptor.com/

Navy's Blue Angels Precision Aerobatic Team
http://www.blueangels.navy.mil/

Origin of the Wild Weasels
http://www.nationalmuseum.af.mil/factsheets/factsheet.asp?id=3666

Silent Eagle: Newest Version of the F-15
http://www.flightglobal.com/news/articles/cutaway-technical-description-how-boeing-developed-the-f-15-silent-eagle-367978/

Vertical Landing of an F-35 Lightning II
http://www.youtube.com/watch?v=-z3glzZuY14

Index

Photo Credits

All images used in this book that are not in the public domain are credited in the listing that follows.

6-7:   Courtesy of Rob Shenk

12:      Courtesy of Kevinalbania

17:      Courtesy of James Dale

39:      Courtesy of Nick Seibert

50:      Courtesy of Alexandr Chechin

61:      Courtesy of Major Paul Greenberg / DVIDS